LIFE IN A
MEDIEVAL CASTLE

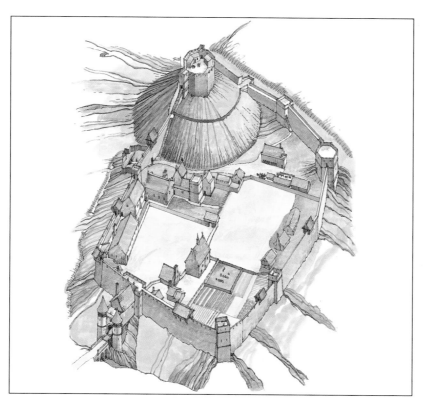

JANE SHUTER

Heinemann Library
Chicago, Illinois

Customer Service 888-454-2279
Visit our website at www.heinemann classroom.com

Originated by Modern Age
Printed in China by WKT Company Limited

09 08 07 06 05
10 9 8 7 6 5 4 3 2 1

Library of Congress Cataloging-in-Publication Data

Shuter, Jane.
  Life in a medieval castle / Jane Shuter.
      p. cm. -- (Picture the past)
  Includes bibliographical references and index.
  ISBN 1-4034-6445-6 (hc) -- ISBN 1-4034-6452-9 (pb)
  1. Castles--Juvenile literature. 2. Civilization, Medieval--Juvenile
literature. I. Title. II. Series.
  GT3550.S48 2004
  940.1--dc22
                                                                2004025845

Acknowledgements:
The publishers would like to thank the following for permission to reproduce photographs: AKG p. 7 (British Library), **18** (British Library), **26** (British Library); Art Archive p. 8 (Cumulus); British Library pp. **9**, **13**, **14**, **28**; Corbis pp. **17** (Archivo Icongrafico, S.A./Corbis), **19**, **20** (RF); Jane Shuter p. 24 (both); Richard Butcher & Magnet Harlequin pp. **6** (Harcourt Education Ltd), **10** (Harcourt Education Ltd), **16** (both Harcourt Education Ltd), **22** (Harcourt Education Ltd).

Cover photograph of a painting of a castle being attacked reproduced with permission of AAAC.

Every effort has been made to contact copyright holders of any material reproduced in this book. Any omissions will be rectified in subsequent printings if notice is given to the publishers.

The paper used to print this book comes from sustainable resources.

Any words appearing in bold, **like this**, are explained in the Glossary.

Contents

Medieval Castles 4
War 6
Building a Castle 8
Changing Castles 10
The Land Around 12
Who Lived in Castles? 14
Castle Supplies 16
Family Life 18
Religion 20
Staying Warm 22
Staying Clean and Healthy .24
Food and Drink 26
Getting Around 28
Glossary 30
Further Reading 31
Index 32

Medieval Castles

Throughout history people have fought each other. So they made their towns and villages safer by building fences or ditches around them. Starting in about 850 C.E., during the **medieval** period, people in Europe built castles, or defended homes just for a **lord** and his **household**. The lord, his family, and his servants and soldiers all lived there. All the land and castles belonged to the king, but the lord could live in the castle as long as he was loyal to the **king**.

Look for these: The gatehouse shows you the subject of each chapter. The helmet shows you boxes with interesting facts, figures, and quotes about life in a castle.

TIMELINE OF EVENTS IN THIS BOOK

850 C.E. First castles in Europe, made from wood

950 C.E. First stone castles in Europe, in France

1066 C.E. William of Normandy invades England and begins building castles there

1100 C.E.   1200 C.E.

CASTLES ARE BUILT WITH TWO WALLS AROUND THE BAILEY 1100–1200 C.E.

850 C.E.

1069 C.E. Bayeux Tapestry begun

1096-1291 C.E. A series of wars, called the Crusades, between Christians and Muslims in the Middle East

This diagram shows how the **feudal system** worked. It shows how medieval lords and rulers kept control of their land and people.

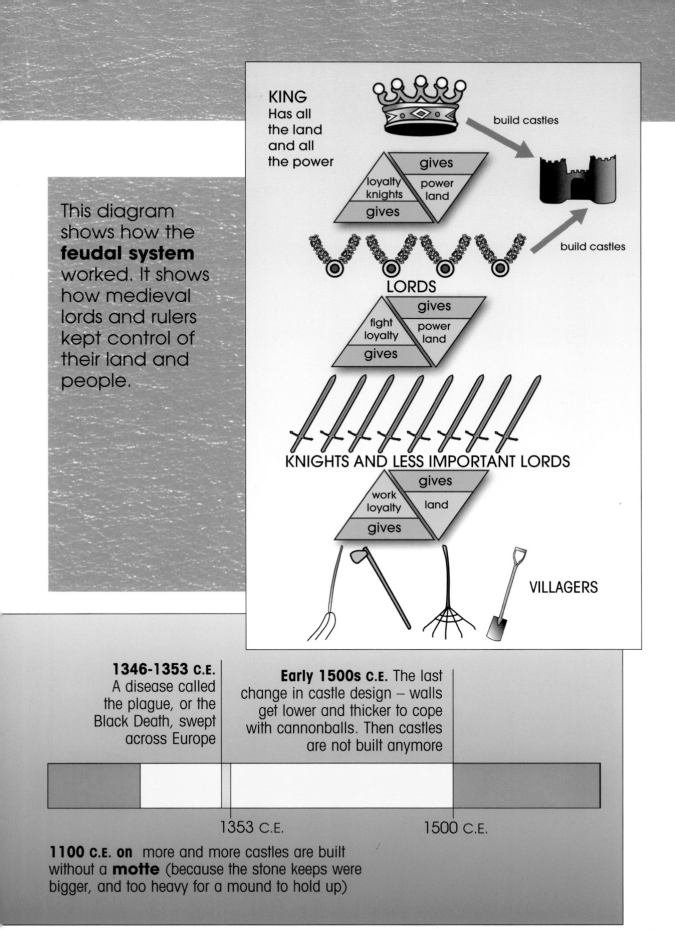

KING
Has all the land and all the power

build castles

gives

loyalty
knights

power
land

gives

build castles

LORDS

gives

fight
loyalty

power
land

gives

KNIGHTS AND LESS IMPORTANT LORDS

gives

work
loyalty

land

gives

VILLAGERS

1346-1353 C.E. A disease called the plague, or the Black Death, swept across Europe

Early 1500s C.E. The last change in castle design — walls get lower and thicker to cope with cannonballs. Then castles are not built anymore

1353 C.E.

1500 C.E.

1100 C.E. on more and more castles are built without a **motte** (because the stone keeps were bigger, and too heavy for a mound to hold up)

War

During the **medieval** period there was always fighting somewhere in Europe. Some were small wars between local **lords**. Others were big wars that involved many countries. Most **kings** and lords had people fight for them. Under the **feudal system**, people had to fight for their kings and lords. But some groups of soldiers, called mercenaries, made a living fighting for anyone who paid them.

MERCENARIES

Mercenaries were soldiers who fought for pay, not out of loyalty. They were often good soldiers, but a lord could not always trust them. Some of them changed sides if offered more money.

This gatehouse guards the only way into Carisbrooke Castle, on the Isle of Wight, UK. Like other castles, it was heavily defended.

Castles were important in wartime. They kept the lord and his army safe from attack. They could be used as a base to fight from—the army would come back to the castle at night to eat and sleep. A lord could just wait for the enemy to tire itself out attacking the castle. Then he would attack when they least expected it.

Some of the biggest medieval wars were the Crusades. Attacks on castles during the Crusades went on for months. The attacking army had to camp outside the castle.

Building a Castle

The earliest castles were made of wood. Soldiers could build one of these castles quickly. They built them on a high mound of earth called a **motte**. The motte was usually in a high place, so soldiers could see all around the countryside from it. Castles were often close to road, and river routes.

This is part of the Bayeux Tapestry, which was made to celebrate the Normans taking over England in 1066. It shows the Normans, who have just landed, building a timber castle.

Once a **lord** and his army had taken over, they often built new, stronger castles from stone. These cost a lot and took a long time to build. They needed a lot of workers, called masons, to cut and carve the stone. A master mason was in charge. He designed the castle and organized the huge amount of stone and other supplies the masons needed.

These builders are using wooden frames and a lifting machine called a lewis, which works the same way as a pair of scissors.

Changing Castles

Castles were built differently at different times in the **medieval** period. The first change was from wood to stone. The basic pattern of a castle stayed the same. It had a **keep** on a **motte**, with a walled area of land below, called the **bailey**. But the height and shape of the walls changed as new weapons were made, and people attacked a castle differently.

WHY CHANGE?

The first changes made castles safer. Toward the end of the medieval period, some changes made castles nicer to live in. Living areas were bigger, there were more fireplaces, and windows were bigger to let in more light.

This window has steps up to a window seat. The big window replaced a narrow slit. It had windowpanes and wooden shutters on the inside.

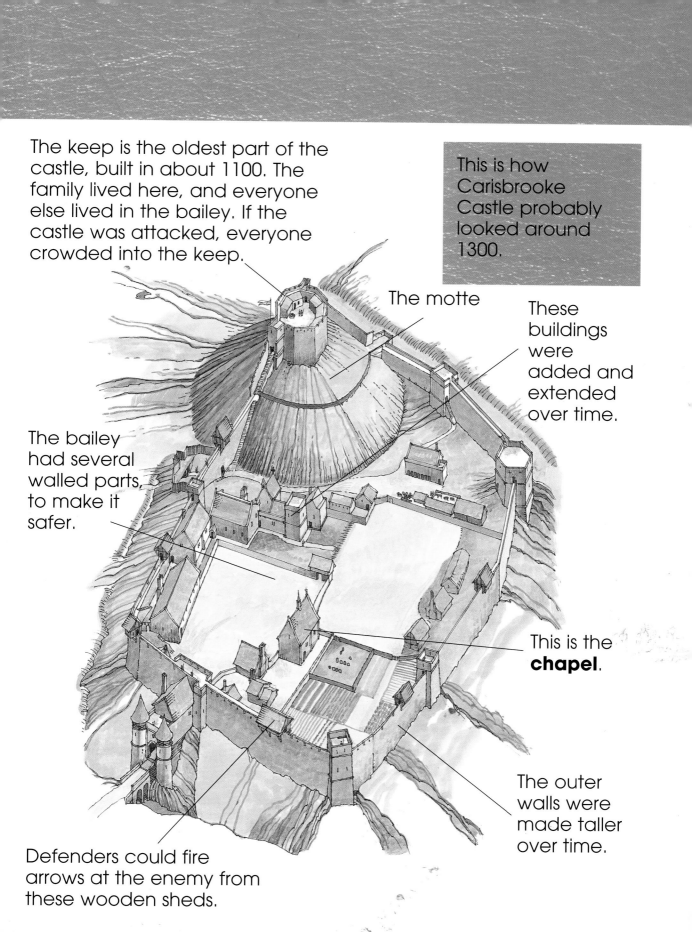

The keep is the oldest part of the castle, built in about 1100. The family lived here, and everyone else lived in the bailey. If the castle was attacked, everyone crowded into the keep.

This is how Carisbrooke Castle probably looked around 1300.

The motte

These buildings were added and extended over time.

The bailey had several walled parts, to make it safer.

This is the **chapel**.

The outer walls were made taller over time.

Defenders could fire arrows at the enemy from these wooden sheds.

The Land Around

Kings gave **lords** land as well as castles. The lands had farms, villages, and even towns. Not all of a lord's land was in the same place. The king might give him land anywhere. But no matter where the lord lived, everyone who lived on his land had to obey him, pay him rent, and work on the land.

DISLOYALTY

A monk writing in 1135 said that disloyal lords in England "built castles against the king. They made local people work on the castles and took everything from the villages. When the villages had no more to give, the lords burned them."

The lord of the castle had to keep his lands, and all the people who lived in them, safe. His knights rode all over his lands to keep control.

Villagers had ties to the village they lived in. Their homes and gardens belonged to the lord, and they were expected to work for the lord for a set number of days a year. In emergencies, the lord could order all the men to go to war for him.

Under the feudal system, villagers had to work hard for the lord. In return, the lord had to keep them safe from attack.

Who Lived in Castles?

The **lord** and his family lived in the castle. The **household** also had soldiers and servants. Many lords had a household of over a hundred people. A **steward** ran the day-to-day life of the castle and the land the lord controlled. He did everything, from making sure meals arrived on time to collecting all the rent.

Servants carried food from the kitchen to the Great Hall where the lord and his family ate. The kitchen was a separate building, so they covered the food to keep it warm.

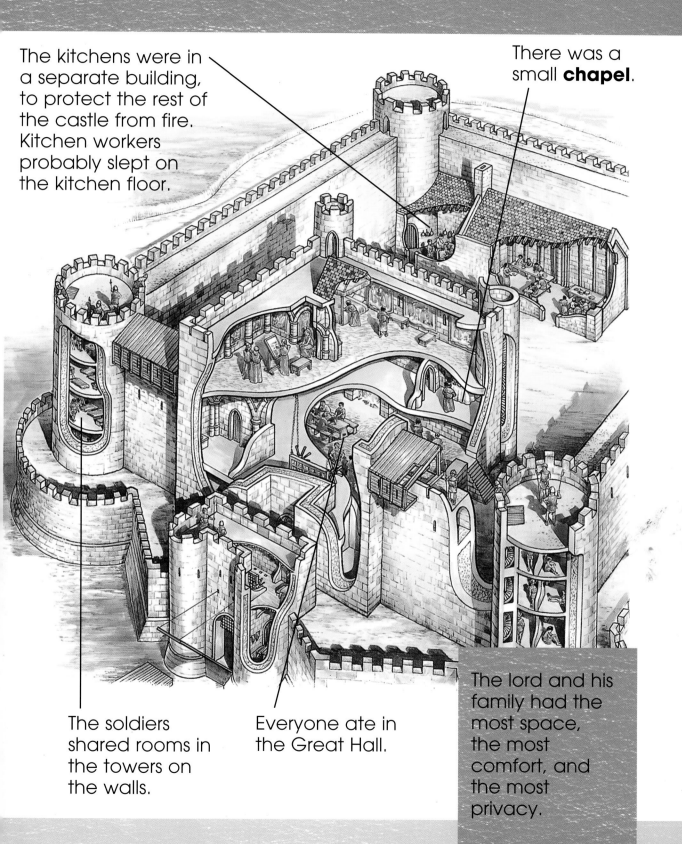

The kitchens were in a separate building, to protect the rest of the castle from fire. Kitchen workers probably slept on the kitchen floor.

There was a small **chapel**.

The soldiers shared rooms in the towers on the walls.

Everyone ate in the Great Hall.

The lord and his family had the most space, the most comfort, and the most privacy.

Castle Supplies

Castles needed a lot of supplies. People used food, drink, candles, **rushes**, and firewood every day. A lot of food came from the farms on the **lord's** land, but expensive food from far away, such as sugar, was bought at big **trading** towns. **Stewards** often ordered supplies for the castle when they were traveling around the lord's land, doing work.

Most castles had a well so that the people could get water if the enemy trapped them inside. There was a well in the **keep** of Carisbrooke Castle, and one below in the **bailey**, so the servants did not have to go up all the steps to the keep just to get water!

Medieval people did not have nearly as much furniture as people do now. They had beds, tables, benches, and a few chests and cupboards to keep clothes, plates, and bowls in. They had far fewer things to store. Even the lord's children only had a few toys.

Tapestries like this hung from the walls of the lord's rooms in the castle. They kept the rooms warmer and added decoration.

Family Life

Everyone in a **medieval** family had different **rights** and **duties**. The father, who was the most important member of the family, had the right to be obeyed by everyone. However, he had the most duties. He had to take care of everyone in his family, and everyone in his **household**, too.

 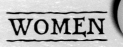
Women in the castle took care of the children and spun and wove cloth to make clothes. Women servants looked after the lord's family and helped to clean the castle and cook.

The woman in the middle is carding wool—combing it with metal teeth to make it straight and smooth. The woman on the left is spinning the carded wool into thread.

Children began to work at about the age of ten. The children of servants learned a job. The sons of the **lord** learned how to ride, fight, and behave at the royal court. His daughters learned how to sing, sew, and dance. Often, the lord's children went to live with another family to learn these skills.

Medieval families did not spend much time together. The lord spent more time with his knights and advisors than he did with his wife and children.

Religion

Most people in Europe during the **medieval** period were **Christians**. At this time, all Christians were Catholic—there was no other Christian religion. All European **kings** saw themselves as part of a big Christian group called Christendom, and loyal to the leader of the Catholic religion, the Pope.

CASTLE CHAPELS

Most castles had their own **chapel**, where the family could pray. Most castles had a priest living there all the time, to run the chapel services.

This chapel is in the Tower of London, one of the first stone castles built in England for William the Conqueror.

Kings and important **lords** wanted to serve God. They often paid to have churches or cathedrals built, or added to, to show how much they respected God. The people who worked on building churches or cathedrals were often the same people who worked on castle building and repairs.

Cathedrals took many years to build. Some builders could spend their whole lives building and repairing one cathedral.

Staying Warm

Castles were cold. Older castles had windows that were just narrow slits in the castle walls. These windows had no glass in them. This made the castle drafty, or windy. There was no such thing as central heating—only fires. There were not many fireplaces through the castle. There was one in the Great Hall, one in the kitchen, and one in the **lord's** private room.

BEDS

Bedrooms did not have fireplaces, so beds had many layers of bedding. The beds of the lord and his family had curtains all around, for privacy and to keep out the drafts.

The kitchen fireplace had small ovens in the back, mostly for making bread.

The lord and the more important people in his household also wore long layers.

All women wore clothes that came down to the ground, such as long dresses.

Servants and other workers wore short tunics, to move around in easily.

The other way people could keep warm was to dress warmly. People wore many layers of clothing, especially the lord and his family. Servants and other workers needed fewer layers of clothing. They kept warm because they were doing hard work all day.

Staying Clean and Healthy

Washing people and clothes was hard work in **medieval** times. There were water tanks in several places in the castle, which were filled with buckets of water from the well. The water was cold, so most people washed in cold water most of the time. Some castles had a laundry room where people washed the clothes. The room often had a fire to heat the water.

BATHS

The **lord** and his family sometimes had a bathtub—a wooden barrel-shaped tub that was filled with water heated on the kitchen fire. It needed to be padded with cloth, so they would not get splinters!

Toilets, called garderobes, stuck out over the outside walls. They had stone seats and a sloping opening that carried everything out and down the walls. People also used pottery containers, which the servants emptied regularly.

Getting sick was dangerous in medieval times. Doctors knew some useful **herbal cures**, and could treat some wounds. But serious wounds, from battles or surgery, often got **infected** and the person died.

People did not know the cause of many diseases. They thought God sent them as punishment. These people beating themselves were called flagellants. They tried to show God how sorry they were for upsetting him, so that he would stop the **plague** that hit Europe in the 1300s.

Food and Drink

Most people ate three or four meals a day. Breakfast was at about 7 A.M. The main meal began at 10 A.M. and lasted until midday. Supper was in the late afternoon. Sometimes people ate something before going to bed. The **lord's** family ate meat every day, as well as white bread and sweet, sugary things. Servants ate mostly brown bread and vegetables. The kitchen workers also got the family's leftovers.

Almost everything was cooked over an open fire, except for bread. Cooks used big metal pots. Some of these could be raised or lowered over the fire. Other pots stood on legs.

Spicy Pork Meatballs

This recipe was the kind of food that was served at a **medieval** feast.

WARNING: Ask an adult to help you with the cooking.

You will need:
1 lb (450g) of spicy pork sausage
1/2 teaspoon of salt
1/2 teaspoon of nutmeg
1/2 teaspoon of powdered cloves
1/2 cup of raisins
3 egg yolks
1/2 teaspoon of tumeric
1 tablespoon of plain flour

1 Pre-heat the oven to 350°F (175°C).

2 Mix the sausage, salt, cloves, nutmeg, and currants together. Roll into balls about the size of a ping-pong ball.

3 Cook the meatballs on a rack over a tray in the oven for 20 minutes. Leave to cool. Put in the fridge for half an hour.

4 Mix the egg yolks with the tumeric and flour to make a paste as thick as toothpaste (you may need more flour).

5 Pre-heat the oven again to 350°F (175°C).

6 Dip the cold pork balls into the paste to cover them. Bake for 15 minutes.

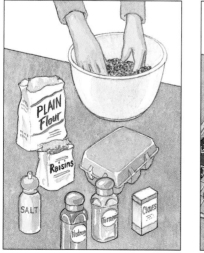

Getting Around

Travel was difficult and dangerous in **medieval** times. Roads were usually just mud paths. They were muddy in winter, and hard and bumpy in summer. Heavy things were carried on roads by carts. Poor people walked. Wealthier people, who could afford to keep a horse, rode.

WHO TRAVELED?

Many people traveled short distances to local markets. Very few people made long journeys. **Traders**, **pilgrims**, and soldiers often traveled long distances. **Stewards** traveled to run the lands belonging to their **lord**.

One of the fastest ways to move around in medieval times was to travel by sea. It was an especially good way to carry heavy **goods**.

Ladies traveled in a traveling carriage, which was like a huge cart filled with cushions and covered with a decorated cloth. Even in the carriage, the ride was still bumpy.

Soldiers marched, unless they were knights, who fought on horseback. Knights rode. Soldiers carried all their weapons and equipment while marching. Armies brought carts with them to carry their supplies.

Glossary

bailey lower part of the castle, inside the castle walls, but not on top of the motte

chapel place to pray

Christian person who believes in the teachings of Jesus Christ and believes that he is the son of God

duty something you are expected to do

feudal system system where the king gives land to lords in return for loyalty, and the lords give land to workers

goods things that are made, bought, and sold

herbal cure medicine made from plants

household all the people living in one place and obeying the same lord

infected when germs get into a wound and cause disease

keep strongest part of a castle, at its center

king ruler of a country

lady wife of a lord

lord ruler of an area of land

medieval period in European history between about 800 and 1500

motte a high mound of earth, made to have a keep built on top

pilgrim person who travels to visit a place that is important in their religion

plague widespread disease

right something you can expect people to do for you

rush plant that grows near a river and has long stems and leaves. These were picked and dried and then thrown onto the stone floors of castles to soak up the spills and dirt.

steward person who runs a lord's castle and lands for him

trade this can mean:
1 job
2 selling or swapping goods

Further Reading

Books

Art of the Middle Ages, Jennifer Olmstead (Heinemann Library, 2001)

The Age of Castles: Castles Under Siege, Richard Dargie (Raintree, 1998)

The Age of Castles: Knights and Castles, Richard Dargie (Raintree, 1998)

The Middle Ages, Mary Quigley (Heinemann Library, 2003)

Index

bailey 10, 11, 16
baths 24
Bayeux tapestry 4, 8
bedrooms 22
building castles 8–9

Carisbrooke Castle 6, 11, 16
chapels 11, 15, 20
children 17, 19
Christians 20
churches and cathedrals 21
cloth-making 18
clothes 23, 24
cooking 26
Crusades 4, 7

defending castles 11
doctors 25
drawbridge 15

family life 18–19
feasts 27
feudal system 5, 6, 12, 13
fireplaces 22
food and drink 14, 16, 26–27
furniture 17

gatehouses 6
Great Hall 14, 15, 22

households 4, 14, 18

keep 10, 11, 16
kings 4, 5, 6, 12, 20, 21
kitchens 14, 15, 22, 26
knights 5, 29

lands 12–13, 28
living areas 10, 15, 17, 22
lords 4, 5, 6, 7, 9, 12, 13, 14, 21, 22, 23, 24, 26

masons 9
mercenaries 6
moats 15
motte 5, 8, 10, 11

plague 5, 25
portcullis 15

religion 20–21
rights and duties 18

servants 4, 14, 16, 18, 19, 23, 26
sickness 25
soldiers 4, 6, 8, 14, 15, 28, 29
spicy pork meatballs 27
stewards 14, 16, 28
stone castles 4, 9, 20
supplies 16–17

tapestries 17
timber castles 4, 8
toilets 24
Tower of London 20
travel 28–29

villages 12, 13

war 6–7, 13, 25
warm, keeping 22–23
washing 24
water supplies 16, 24
wells 16, 24
windows 10, 22
women 14, 18, 23, 29